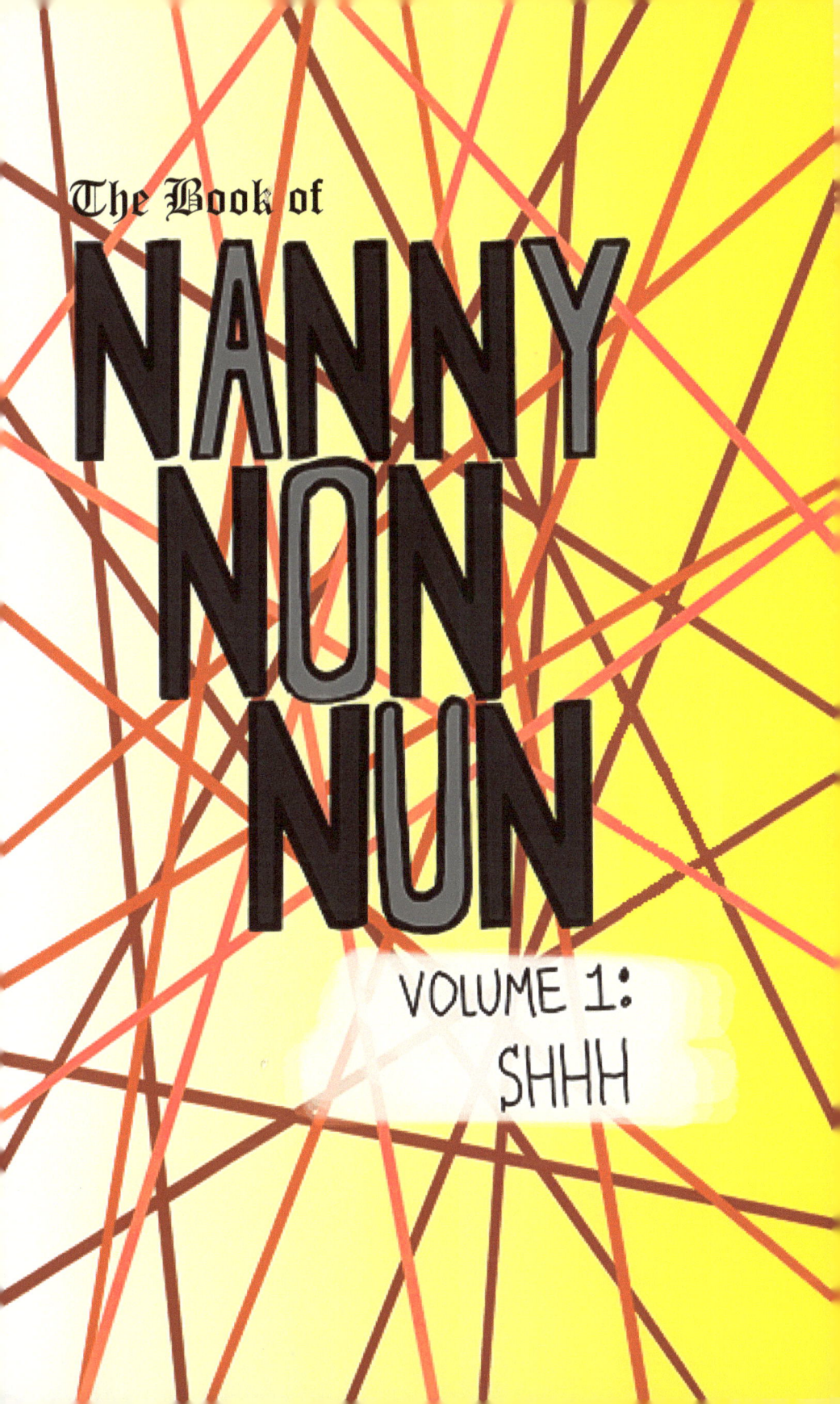

The Book of Nanny Non Nun Volume 1: SHHH
Copyright 2021 by Leather & Leaf Books Publishing
Written by Nanny Non Nun, Minneapolis Minnesota
ALL RIGHTS RESERVED. No part of this book may be distributed or reproduced in any manner, what so ever, without expressed written permission of the author. Address ALL inquires to:
LeatherandLeafBooks@gmail.com
ISBN # 978-1-7362197-3-7
All Writing, Illustrations and Layout Design done by Nanny Non Nun

WARNING

+18

    I, Nanny Non Nun,
am a strict disciple and vessel for God. This collection is a gospel of God's tongue spitting through my veiny hands, to ink; a peek into his deepest thoughts and salacious secrets of the Pope's tier. As the strong left back hand of God I am but a tool in the grand scheme of heavenly plans and it is my duty, my burden, to share the visions. So reader beware; only those of lost, or lots of, faith fare well.

NNN

Safety Word

If safety is something you seek,
I hold the key to your Sanctuary.
Fall on your knees,
and give me please.
Body falls weak taken into my Oratory.

A magic phrase leading you to perish,
With your body as the shrine.
But don't forget,
Say it LOUD!
If you're not of the herd; you're mine!

AAAAAAAAAA!!!!!

Strapped, tied, nailed to my cross.
Nanny Non Nun on a bossy mission.
        Body and soul-
          prey on the alter.
Chance to talk is gone. Just shut up and listen!

Close your eyes, I'll mask your fear.
Secure the fold, my covenant's scary.
        Your hole of glory,
          with every fifth bead.
A rosary to make you hale Mary.

Stole your square position, kept you from pew.
I'm the ruler and it's time to measure the knuckle.
        My offered hand
          Enters your haven.
My collared father crying until you're yelling...
                    'Pineapple'.

EEEEEEEEE!!!!!

Master Class

All my pleasures put aside,
Only my student's, I abide.
A teacher first.
I shelf the thirst.
Gender pref. or personal kink,
I'll hide.

Tell me what you yearn,
A confession mine to earn.
Rubber? Leather? Fur?
Pain or shame sufferer.
From pure to sex-sure,
you're going to learn.

Klink like plink-o-chips,
Hitting all pegs with no skips.
Scratching every itch.
And if you miss a pitch.
I'll switch up plans, in time,
for double dips.

A session from an expert.
Sweet vanilla extract squirt.
　　　Sugar cookie intake,
　　　　big rookie mistake.
Frenzy break to soften gravity's hurt.

You strictly masturbate?
You're ace or maybe celi-bate?
　　　You'll find out quick,
　　　　If it's not your shtick.
My angle will be done at any rate.

Quick bottoms and tops that linger,
an S&M couple or single swinger.
　　　Dabble; Try it all;
　　　　become professional.
An array of pies ready for my finger.

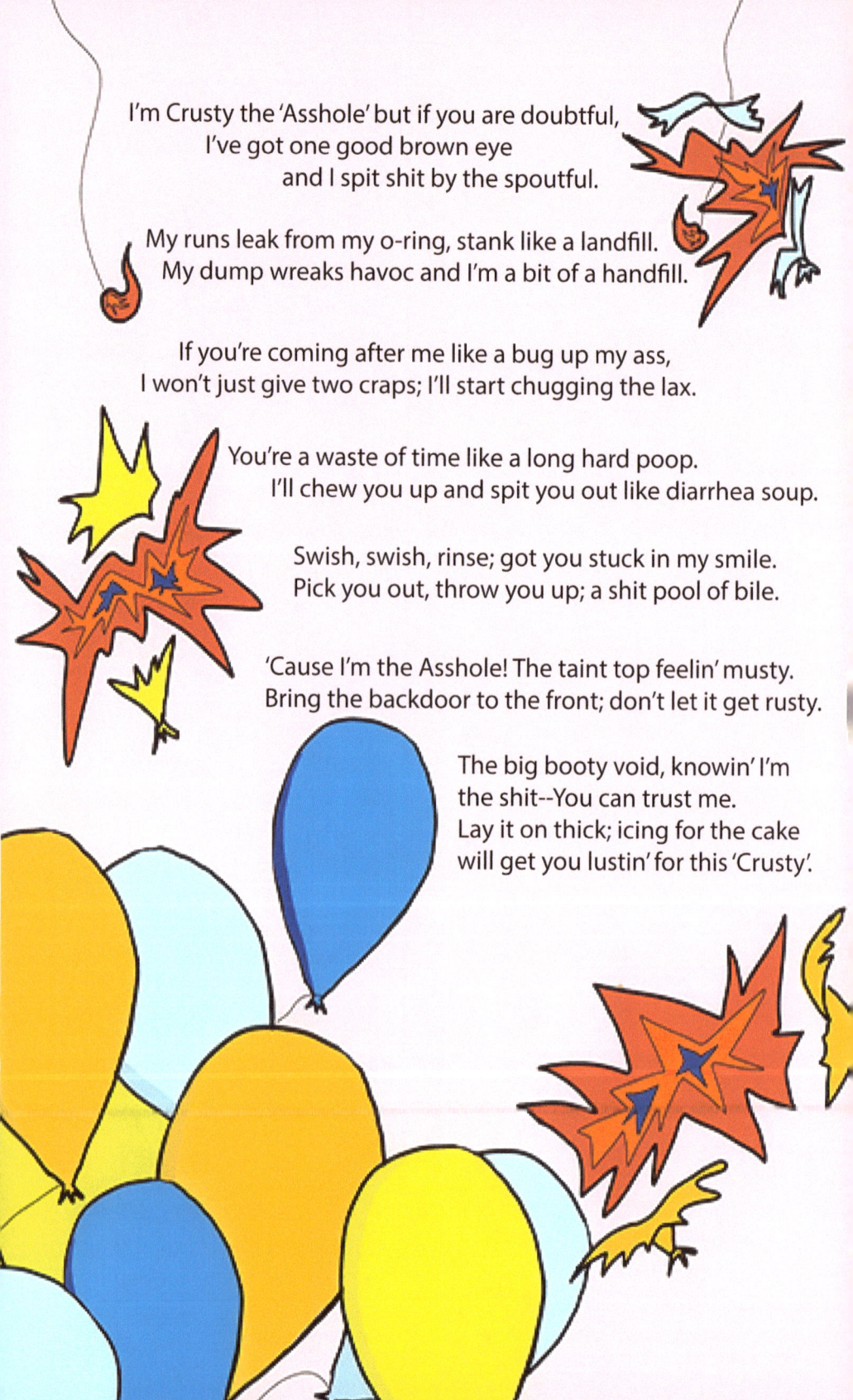

I'm Crusty the 'Asshole' but if you are doubtful,
I've got one good brown eye
and I spit shit by the spoutful.

My runs leak from my o-ring, stank like a landfill.
My dump wreaks havoc and I'm a bit of a handfill.

If you're coming after me like a bug up my ass,
I won't just give two craps; I'll start chugging the lax.

You're a waste of time like a long hard poop.
I'll chew you up and spit you out like diarrhea soup.

Swish, swish, rinse; got you stuck in my smile.
Pick you out, throw you up; a shit pool of bile.

'Cause I'm the Asshole! The taint top feelin' musty.
Bring the backdoor to the front; don't let it get rusty.

The big booty void, knowin' I'm
the shit--You can trust me.
Lay it on thick; icing for the cake
will get you lustin' for this 'Crusty'.

Holy Plead

Breathe on me
Holy Spirit.
For you, I've kept myself lonely.
Horny, for you, I pray to hear it.
One and Only
Holy Spirit.

Leaking holy water. Can you cure it?
Come fuck me, Holy Spirit.

Don't leave me virgin.
I want to rear it.
Suck me to Heaven

Holy Spirit.

Your Godly silence,
I fear it.
My dream, Holy Spirit.
Fill me up with holy cream.
Then I'll sit on your Halo
to help you clear it.

Holy Guacamole.

Snowballed
into sacrament.
Face covered
in semen,
spirited assent.

Amen

Lord's Addition

My daddy,
You, too, can come in.
Let me scream thy name
I quiver within.
Finding my zen.
A threesome with Spirit
and Him
Amen

Give me the son.
Oh! Then I cum.
Giving praise every
hit of the rim.
Amen

And foreplay includes eating asses,
as we finger those who eat the ass
for the masses.
Amen

And
lead us 'round
with a dildo cross
but deliver unto me
the holy sauce.
Amen

For thine is all I think,
and my lust,
and my kink,
forever in head,
in bed.

Amen
and
Amen
again.

Curly Q

If my bush and pit and the hair from my head tip,

All tangled
And wrangled
And strangled together.

I'd cough and spit from all the hair I emit.

I'd sneeze
And wheeze
And seize up together.

I'd push and lift to control the hair fit.

But its grizzled,
And twizzled,
And frizzled together.

I'd grab brush and pick and comb the hair slick.

To be faded,
And separated,
And braided together.

WANTED AD

Wanted;
In search of a house maid.
Must do;
EVERYTHING for my aide,
Only.

I'll give:
The required supplies;
Odd tools it will comprise,
Knee pads and a kinky disguise.

You'll have;
Prepared,
All your credentials please.
Lube; in form of elbow grease.
Pig tails, short skirt – foot from the knees.

Preferred,
For ease;
A miss that takes the piss.
A mouth big enough for fists.
Two fists at least up to the wrists.

Reply,
Like this,
"I can polish your doorknobs.
Feather knick-knacks, bits and bobs,
Wipe, mop, suck and tend to all your jobs.
No probs."

Sub Offered

Answ'ring
Yesterday's house maid ad.
Choose me;
I'm up to clean your pad.

Response
you want:
"Slick doorknobs are a breeze.
Dusting do-dads? What a tease.
I'll do ANY task"…we'll talk fees.

I'll need,
at least,
Two additional suits,
Thigh high studded leather boots.
Mouths only wide if you'll eat fruits.

Send for-
the miss?
Skirt or dress, I'll wear less.
For your request, I'll make a 'yes'.
So, get the best; to get no mess.

I'm Miss-
ter D. Stress.
Miss or sir, all the above.
In spandex, tight like a glove.
The only sex you'll see is love;
Lots of.

Inflated

Hung balls.
        Two balls.
                Free balls.
                        Blue balls.
Lights out.
        Loose wrists.
                Soft breath.
                        Tight grips.
Head pokes.
        Fluid soaks.
                Harder chokes.
                        Faster Strokes.
White eyes.
        Hard sighs.
                Twitching thighs.
                        Lustful cries.
Heaving slow.
        Toes roll.
                Sweaty glow.
                        About to blow.
Body fun.
        Over run.
                Loaded gun.
                        Glazed precum.
Jacking it;
        near eruption.
                FUCKING SHIT!!!
                        ...an interruption...

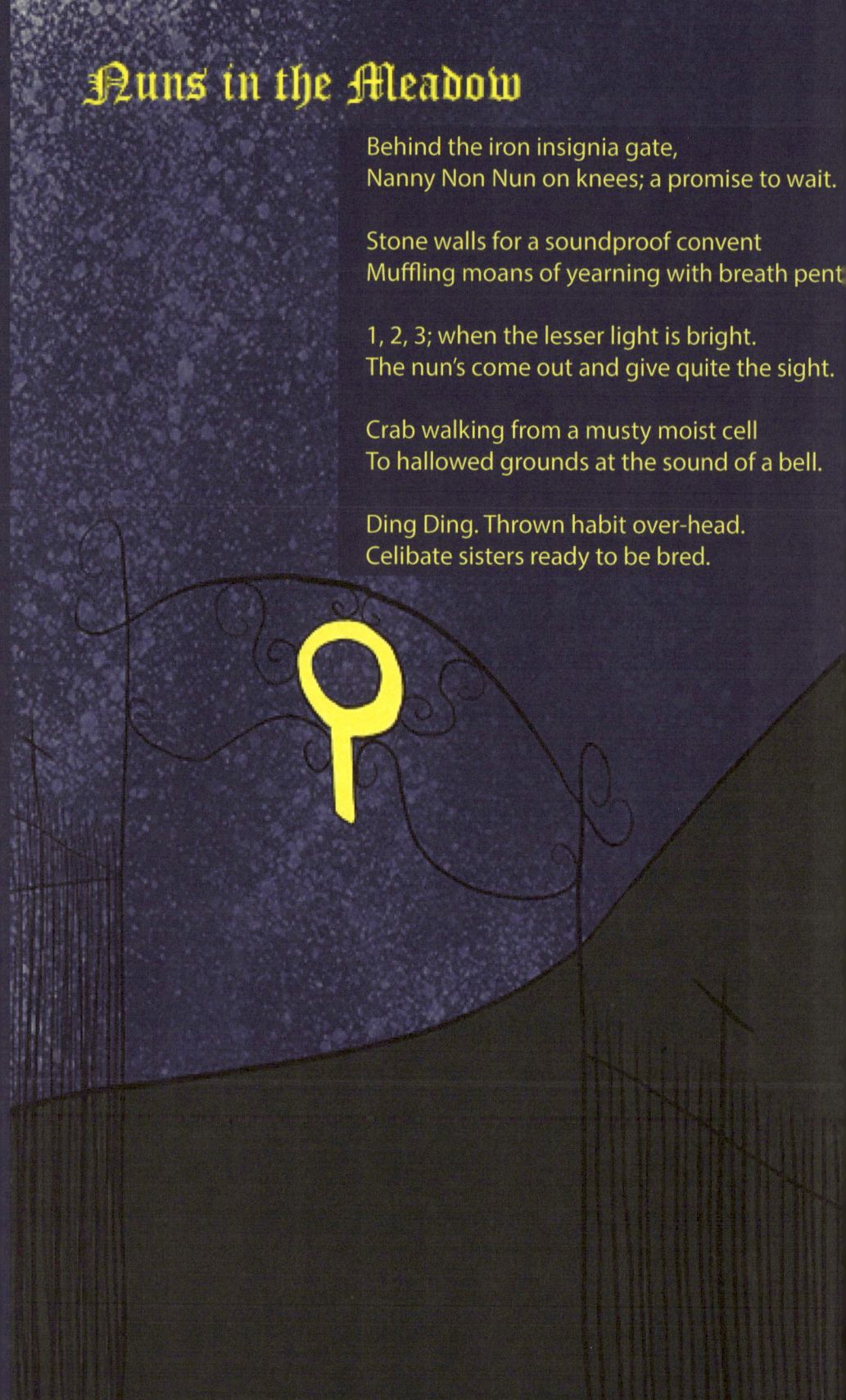

Nuns in the Meadow

Behind the iron insignia gate,
Nanny Non Nun on knees; a promise to wait.

Stone walls for a soundproof convent
Muffling moans of yearning with breath pent

1, 2, 3; when the lesser light is bright.
The nun's come out and give quite the sight.

Crab walking from a musty moist cell
To hallowed grounds at the sound of a bell.

Ding Ding. Thrown habit over-head.
Celibate sisters ready to be bred.

Bridge pose for a perineum moon bath.
Like vaginas in rapture rushing to God's wrath.

Concentrated beams for Jehovah's donation shot.
Between thighs, a slit of lunar rays caught.

Quivered orgasms saved for the master.
Like an unchastised bull put out to pasture.

Dawn will come with blessed after dew on grass.
Proof of their lay? The hand of God left on ass.

Don't be confused by our sexual acts versus our purity pacts.
We separate business from pleasure.
Our 'job', to pound out the sin from within.
Our 'joy', to keep our pussies a treasure.

Trans' Plans

Let the trans-hu-man have plans to trans;
From old hu-man to new hu-man.
Just like you can,
When you plan for plans from hands of man's
without the "Can I plan?" ask, from trans.
Don't scan the past hu-man plans,
When the new trans hu-man needs no exam.
And if the tran's future plans goes trans a-gains?
Don't stand for bans from hateful clan hands.
Understand?

There's a stub
on my bum thumb's nub.
Some bub presumbed
my stub was my thumb
and my bum thumb was a nub.
To the bub, I sud,
"It's a stubbed nub on a bum thumb.
Not a nubbed thumb; or a thumb sub."
Then the bub sud,
"Welcome cub!
Join the club and grab some grub."
The bub then showed his stub
on his bum thumb nub
and opened the door
to the 'Nub Thumb Pub Hub'
I sud,
"Well done!"
to the bub upon welcome
into the fun bum thumb club.
Inside the pub,
the bum thumb club
had 'rub-a-stub' fun in a tub of grub
A bum to be dubbed with
'The best thumb stub on a nub-bub';
                      I won!

A
Sore
Thumb
War
Score

The Fester System

Rumor has it, came from eight,
Left for dead right out the gate.
Grown up in the church. Oh! What a fate!
Taught by the Nuns to hate the hate.

                                        From runt to a fitted frame.
                                        Shift shame; abuse and blame.
                                        Take the anger; learn to tame.
                                        Now a hired hand to claim.

                    Sinners gone astray; my pray
                    Don't lose your way or I'll slay.
                    But won't die today if there's pay.
                    Instead taken by tray; a market fillet.

Suggestions to stay alive:
Fly like the nuns of the hive.
To Father, make the divine dive.
You'll find strive for a lively thrive.

                                  Live sin and get the latch-or
                                  Whatever prison hatcher.
                                  The nuns are the spirit matcher
                                  but for your sins...
                                  I'm the body 'Snatcher'.

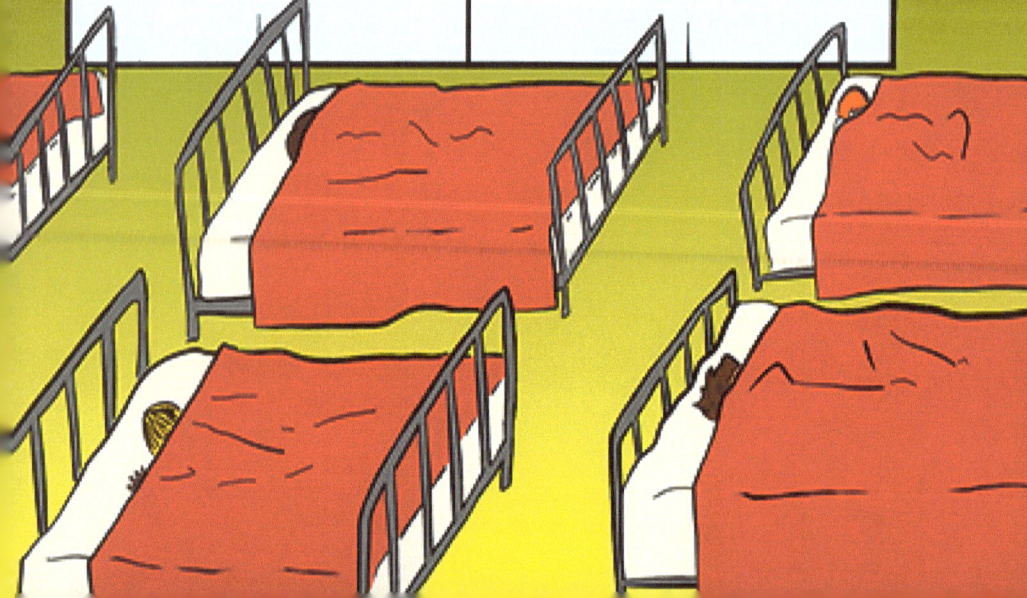

Sister's of Nazareth, the Nuns;
Keeping Jesus in their bloodline runs.
Using the lore from past generations,
And a ritual used with the wombs of virgins.
Pushing sex to the masses by the tons.
Highlighting the importance of daughters and sons;
But behind the closed doors of these charlatans.
They practice their own unpreached lessons.
Saving the good vagina like fine porcelains.
Unfolded only by the hands of the head Artisan's.

S.O.N.S

Church Chess

Profits prophets! They will come to us!
Hymn Him! And gain trust.
Give them a place in which to congregate.
They'll be back every week to seal their fate.

Hear Here! We can control God's power.
Our Hour! They will cower.
"Sit down. Stand up. Bow to the cross."
A filter to capture the praise for the boss.

Flower Power

Upright! Set Tight!
From lip to lip, no teeth insight.
Low height! Just right!
From hip to hip. Ready to fight!

Slam! Bam! Pow, Pow, POW!
Left! Right! Left! Right!
Ignite your might!

Wham! Damn! Wow, Wow, WOW!
Left! Right! Left! Right!
Incite your excite!

Smite the slight
to enlighten your bright!
Despite the blight
or contrite white knight.

Yet, Unite!
Alright with the polite
insight to overwrite
the uptight plight
from societal fright.

                    Recite.

Coarse Course! To fester the guilt.
Kneed need! Indoctrinated fear built.
Constant uneasy rest from a fiery beast,
But don't let them see the leash held by the priest.

Baa Baa! When the wolf owns the sheep.
"Bless sir, Bless sir." Wolf puts them to sleep.
The herd is weakened. Resources willingly stole.
Wolves living in splendor and coughing up wool.

Idle Idol! Position for a plan.
Morning Mourning! Masters of the middleman.
Hiding the thought of the most powerful creator-
Needing the help of a mansplaining translator.

My Ass Hats

I have a laughy grass ass hat,
with packs of grassy wax to smash
and gas during a laughy bash.

I've got a brass ass hat
for brassy lassy catz who asks to dance
to badass cat's brass.

My sassy ass hat is too crass
for most tasks but takes a fast axe
for hashing facts when a sassy ass
wants to bask and relax.

From frats to brats my trash ass hat
will match the masses.
But for hacks to pass and outlast,
I grasp my class act ass hat.
That racks the clicks and clacks!

Poket Pusy Vilov

Fart odors bothering your homes?
Embarrassed of sharts?
This spongy creature eats smells
as it roams for musty gas darts.

The floating
'Flatus Heteractis'!
These air anemones,
With tentacles,
hair and spikes like catties.
It even sweeps chimneys.

It sucks up
and converts fresh rips.
The booty's sours,
Digesting particles
to nectar drips.
Like sweet flowers.

But don't sniff
at the honey trap's sips.
Poses roses.
Meant to lure bugs,
but found in its grips,
Clipped tips of curious noses.

Change the tag, rip off the label.
Muscles in dresses! Everyone's able!

Some of this; None of that. We are all unique.
Whatever you are made of, give them all a peek.

Without variety we can only find homo-geneous.
Take the mix, and throw it in. More ingredients!

1 to 10? Looks don't make men.
Fragile as a daisy, doesn't make a lady.

You cannot mimic, copy or paste, another somebody.
You decide, what's inside and
how to express what you embody.

Duties

Nanny Non Nun the church's spire,
Needs a display of the skills she requires.
Take a broom handle.
The wax of a candle.
Blood, sweat and elbow grease from the hires.

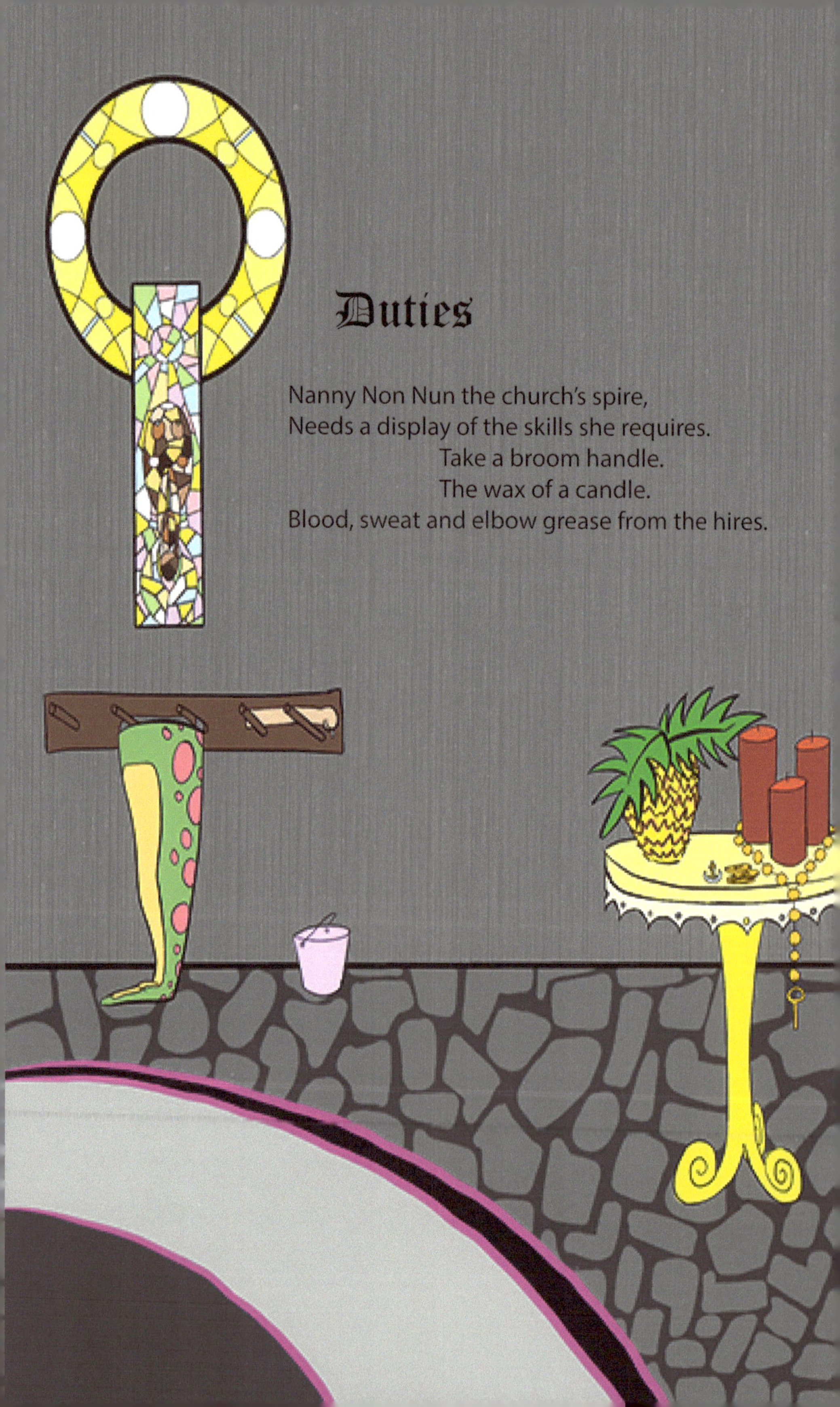

Temple topping with pew bottom play.
Cross pegged with a secret handshake spray.
　　　　Rubber heel worship.
　　　　Pentagram rope grip.
Soo pleased; you'll give your rib away.

The god box a throne for queening.
Give your second cumming a 'trinity' meaning.
　　　　Pennant edging.
　　　　Fetish blessing.
Lock on the halo handcuffs and get to deep cleaning.

Swab down the Sister's mason racks.
Sanitize the angel suspension slacks.
　　　　A fresh plastic sheet.
　　　　Everything back to neat.
Punctually back again on Sunday night
　　　　　　to wipe those dirty cracks.

A Cock Fight

Cock on cock.
Yanked off sock.
Beats on lock.
Prepare the doc.

Skin in the game,
Shouting my name.
Adding the pain.
Handing out blame.

Claw and hit.
Papercut the slit.
Rise up and spit.
Weave and bob it.

My odds, the best!
Giving nothing less.
Flaccid and boneless.
Left a hot mess.

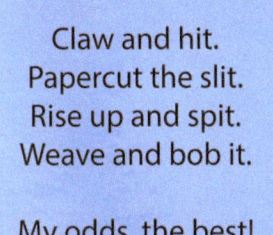

Soaked

Sinking in deeper and deeper
Salty waters, temperature increasing.
Embrace tightening, gripping all around.
Feeling of wonder; inhibitions releasing.

Through the darkness a creature emerges.
Just a glimpse at first, hiding out of sight.
Then 1 sucker, 10 suckers,
100 suckers from the shadows take flight.

They cling to my deep diving suit.
Searching my body for any way in.
Breaking the seams and slipping up and under,
Thick, throbbing, tentacles wrapping my skin.

I hold my breath as the air turns to water.
My protection drifting away…
Squid fingers probing my lips.
They force their way in…to my dismay.

The full monster comes in the light,
Once its prey is on its knees.
It's excitement to eat hurts.
I feel the arms inside me tense and squeeze.

Helplessly, gagged and bound.
All my holes are filled.
Tears in the water mix,
With the saliva from the gilled.

As the jaws come down, I wake up.
I am safe and I rejoice.
But I swear my bed was dry before I slept;
And now it is all moist.

Diary Page 1 from on High

God knows all yet slept with the enemy.
Surprised enough to break his trust
and blind the 'King of Kings' with singing lust.
His best in show; a trick con melody.

Deceit, backstabbed, but Jah still favored Lu.
A scorned-up love too pained to face their ex.
Jah gave Lu land, a throne and crew, best specs.
and halted changing heart, left Lu to stew.

I always dreamt of my own wild vineyard.
I, Gab, shall toot Jah's horn and win first chair.
If blowing works, we'd make a brassy pair.
If not? Lu got hell. Get me my reward.

Bring back Eden and leave me on the Earth.
Heaven leads up this way, Hell leads astray.
Adamah best for learning AND for play.
Soo bored above, a need for change, rebirth.

Gabriel

www.ingramcontent.com/pod-product-compliance
Lightning Source LLC
Chambersburg PA
CBHW041808160426
43209CB00016B/1726